3 4028 07342 3098
HARRIS COUNTY PUBLIC LIBRARY

J 363.25 Har
Harris, Nathaniel
Crime fighting : the impact
of science and technology

North A   D1544715

WITHDRAWN

Pros and Cons

CRIME FIGHTING

The Impact of Science and Technology

Nathaniel Harris

Gareth Stevens
Publishing

Please visit our web site at: www.garethstevens.com.
For a free color catalog describing Gareth Stevens Publishing's list of high-quality books, call 1-800-542-2595 (USA) or 1-800-387-3178 (Canada). Gareth Stevens Publishing's fax: 1-877-545-2596

Library of Congress Cataloging-in-Publication Data

Harris, Nathaniel, 1937-
    Crime fighting : the impact of science and technology / by Nathaniel Harris.
        p. cm. — (Pros and cons)
    Includes bibliographical references and index.
    ISBN-10: 1-4339-1985-0   ISBN-13: 978-1-4339-1985-5 (lib. bdg.)
    1. Criminal investigation—Juvenile literature. I. Title.
HV8073.8.H37 2010
363.25—dc22   2009012433

This North American edition published in 2010 by Gareth Stevens Publishing under license from Arcturus Publishing Limited.
Gareth Stevens Publishing
A Weekly Reader® Company
1 Reader's Digest Road
Pleasantville, NY 10570-7000 USA

Copyright © 2009 Arcturus Publishing Limited
Produced by Arcturus Publishing Limited
26/27 Bickels Yard
151-153 Bermondsey Street
London SE1 3HA

Gareth Stevens Executive Managing Editor: Lisa M. Herrington
Gareth Stevens Editors: Jayne Keedle, Joann Jovinelly
Gareth Stevens Senior Designer: Keith Plechaty

Series Concept: Alex Woolf
Editor and Picture Researcher: Nicola Barber
Cover Design: Phipps Design
Consultant: Miles Hudson

Picture Credits: Corbis: 8 (Brooks Kraft), 11 (Bettmann), 12 (Digital Art), 13 (Jerry McCrea/*The Star Ledger*), 16 (Andy Rain/epa),19 (Alessia Pierdomenico/Reuters), 30 (Yahya Arhab/epa), 32 (Narendra Shrestha/epa), 46 (Gideon Mendel), 48 (Jerome Sessini); Rex Features: 52 (Giles Moberly/PYMCA); Science Photo Library: Cover (Pasieka), 5 (Philippe Psaila), 22 (George Steinmetz), 29 (Photo Researchers), 35 (Michael Donne, University of Manchester), 36 (Mauro Fermariello), 39 (Michel Viard, Peter Arnold, Inc.), 43 (Dr. Jurgen Scriba), 44 (Tek Image), 50 (Ted Kinsman), 55 (Andrew Brookes, National Physical Laboratory), 59 (Charles D. Winters); Shutterstock: 7 (Dusan Po), 15 (Mikael Damkier), 21 (Pres Panayotov), 25 (Gary Blakeley), 26 (Gary Yim), 41 (Benjaminet), 57 (Yuyangc).

Cover: A computer-generated image of a glowing handprint shows its individual details. Just as fingerprints are unique to each person, palm prints can also be used to link possible suspects to crime scenes.

Every attempt has been made to clear copyright. Should there be any inadvertent omission, please apply to the publisher for rectification.

All rights reserved.

Printed in the United States

1 2 3 4 5 6 7 8 9 15 14 13 12 11 10 09

CONTENTS

CHAPTER 1
Science and Crime   4

CHAPTER 2
The Computer Age   10

CHAPTER 3
Watching and Listening   18

CHAPTER 4
Global Threats   26

CHAPTER 5
Questions of Identity   34

CHAPTER 6
In the Line of Duty   46

CHAPTER 7
The Future of Crime Fighting   54

Glossary   60
Further Information   63
Index   64

Science and Crime

On August 4, 1892, 32-year-old Lizzie Borden found her father and stepmother dead in the family home at Fall River, Massachusetts. An apparently frenzied attacker had smashed their heads with repeated ax blows. The Bordens' family had been unhappy, and much of the evidence pointed to Lizzie as the murderer. She was put on trial, but the jury was not quite convinced of her guilt and found her innocent.

The Borden case became one of the United States' most famous unsolved murders. Today, scientific investigators would almost certainly find the conclusive evidence needed to prove or disprove Lizzie's guilt. That might, for example, take the form of microscopic spots of blood, or near-invisible fibers that could be shown to have come from an intruder's clothing — if there was an intruder.

Blood Will Tell

Violent crimes generally leave behind a trail of blood. Crime investigators can learn much from the shapes of blood drops, splashes, and stains. They are often able to reconstruct what happened at the crime scene, including the victim's movements after being struck, or the direction from which he or she was wounded. Every human being has blood that belongs to one of four types. That fact can help prove a person's guilt or innocence. If your blood belongs to a different blood type from that of a wanted criminal, you cannot be that person.

The Crime Scene

Science-based techniques and tools have since transformed the process of criminal investigation. Scientific techniques have not, however, replaced traditional police work, which remains vital. Police officers question witnesses and suspects, take statements, conduct door-to-door investigations, and appeal to the public for information. Police detectives examine what the evidence means, search for motives, and follow leads until they identify and arrest the suspected criminals.

Until the 1950s, detectives took the leading role in investigating crime scenes. The crime scene is the place where a crime has been committed, or any place where useful evidence is discovered. The crime scene is closed off and the first people to enter it are experts wearing white "clean suits," including gloves, masks, and boots. Those uniforms and gear protect experts from on-site infections. The suits also ensure that nothing from the experts' own bodies becomes mixed with evidence. Without such precautions, biological material from an investigator might contaminate the crime scene, or taint useful evidence from it. Contaminated evidence may be rejected in court. Expert photographers record every aspect of the crime scene before investigators may touch anything. Investigators then search for evidence, placing samples of anything movable, such as hair strands or cloth fibers, into bags that are carefully sealed and labeled.

At a crime scene, investigators collect evidence, which is bagged and labeled. The investigators wear protective "clean suits" that protect them from harmful substances and ensure they do not contaminate the scene or its evidence.

If there is a body at the crime scene, a pathologist, or medical examiner, will examine it before it is removed. A pathologist is an expert in identifying cause of death. He or she detects and analyzes diseases and wounds. Later, he or she will perform a post-mortem examination, or autopsy. That is a surgical examination of a dead body to determine how and when the person died, the nature of his or her injuries, and what kind of weapon wounded him or her. Sometimes the pathologist can determine specific details, such as the likely height and build of the attacker.

Back in the laboratory, experts use a variety of scientific resources to extract information from evidence found at the scene. Specialists test samples of blood, hair, and body fluids. Those may prove decisive in identifying who was present at the time. Minute fibers, soil quality, seeds, or even pollen grains may also offer important clues. All substances from the crime scene are analyzed and identified.

Paper Trail

Writing may also provide vital evidence. For example, a handwriting expert can compare a ransom note with a suspect's handwriting and know with fair certainty whether the suspect wrote the note. A blank sheet may provide evidence if it carries impressions of words written on a sheet above it in a notepad. An electrostatic sensitive device (ESD) shows the faintest impressions by forcing toner, a kind of printing ink, into the shallow grooves made by pen pressure. Writing materials can also give away a forgery. In 1983, a journalist named Gerd Heidemann claimed to have discovered the diaries of German dictator Adolf Hitler. The diaries were regarded as a sensational find until analysis showed that both the paper and the ink dated from after Hitler's death in 1945.

Prints and Impressions

Fingerprinting is one of the best-known crime-fighting techniques. Every individual's fingerprints are unique, so their presence at a crime scene is very strong evidence. A fingerprint may be visible in a splatter of blood or mud, but most fingerprints are latent, or invisible, until revealed. The basic

technique for revealing latent fingerprints involves sprinkling surfaces with powder. When blown away, the powder will stick to the slightly oily marks made by fingers, creating a distinctive pattern. Investigators at the crime scene press sticky tape onto the prints, lifting them intact, so that the evidence exists in a more permanent form.

Other impressions may be found at the scene, such as shoe prints and tire tracks. Investigators record those by lifting them like fingerprints if they have been left on a hard surface, or taking casts if they have made an impression on a soft surface, such as mud. To make a cast, plaster or resin is poured into the print. The plaster or resin hardens to make a copy of the impression. The hard cast is removed and shown later, as evidence.

These examples show the intricacy and individuality of fingerprints. The lines are classified into types of patterns, such as arches, loops, and whorls, and may be combined in an infinite number of ways.

Forensic Science

Laboratory-based crime investigating is described as forensic, or law-related, science. Many people have become interested in that subject, largely thanks to popular TV series such as *CSI* (*Crime Scene Investigation*). Forensic science uses many different specialized subjects. A typical example is forensic biology, which might involve examining the flies and other insects that sometimes invade corpses, since their presence indicates how long a person has been dead.

Guns and Bullets

The study of firearms and bullets is known as ballistics. After a shooting, the weapon used is often missing from the crime scene, but police will seize any firearm in the possession of a suspect. Grooves inside the barrel of every gun are different. Those grooves leave unique marks on bullets as they pass through the barrel. Ballistics experts compare the scratches and marks on crime-scene bullets with marks made on bullets test-fired from a suspect's gun. If the marks on the two sets of bullets match, the suspect's gun must have been the weapon used at the crime scene. Analysis of weapons and cartridges (the cases that hold bullets) supply other crucial facts.

A forensic expert in Washington, D.C., studies the marks on a bullet. He wants to learn whether they match those on a bullet fired by a sniper who terrorized the area in 2002. If the marks are identical, the bullets must have been fired by the same weapon.

Forensic science plays its part in many types of investigations. Those may range from the murder of one individual, to war crimes such as genocide, or the mass murder of an entire people. But forensic science contributes to solving many other crimes, such as armed kidnapping, robbery, theft, smuggling, and drug dealing. Highly specialized skills are needed to identify forgeries of old documents, wills, passports, antiques, and even works of art.

Forensic scientists use advanced technology to analyze evidence. For example, the comparison microscope has two microscopes side-by-side that enable scientists to see a split view in order to compare samples without the risk of contaminating them by contact. Powerful scanning electron microscopes magnify objects many thousands of times to show details that cannot be seen with the naked eye. Other instruments use various kinds of light, such as laser beams, infrared, ultraviolet, and X-rays. Those instruments perform a range of tasks from revealing traces of blood to seeing beneath the surface of possibly forged documents or paintings.

 PROS: FORENSIC EVIDENCE

Advanced scientific techniques improve detection rates and make people feel a greater sense of security. The accuracy of scientific analysis increases public confidence that justice is being fairly served.

 CONS: FORENSIC EVIDENCE

Science is unbiased, but humans sometimes make mistakes when applying scientific techniques. Shows such as *CSI* give the impression that any crime can be solved easily and completely. In reality, forensic evidence may be significant but not completely conclusive. Juries may rely too heavily on what they believe to be hard science and react unfavorably when that evidence seems flawed. In 1995, retired American football player O.J. Simpson was accused of murder. Although the case against Simpson was strong, he was acquitted after it was revealed that forensic evidence used in the case had been compromised.

CHAPTER 2

The Computer Age

Computers have revolutionized modern life. A few people used the earliest computers for military and educational purposes, but sales of personal computers (PCs) for home use boomed during the late 1980s. At the same time, networks of linked computers and the Internet vastly increased users' ability to communicate and access information.

By the 1990s, millions of ordinary people used computers for work and pleasure, browsing the Internet, sending e-mails or messaging in chat rooms, shopping, playing games, and transacting business. Today, every large institution or organization relies on computer systems capable of storing, organizing, and sending information at incredibly high speeds.

Computers Against Crime

Computers and computer networks have become equally indispensable as crime-fighting tools. The computer can record and catalog immense databases, organizing facts about crimes, material evidence, and lists of witnesses and suspects. Almost every aspect of forensic science has benefited from being computerized. For example, there are currently millions of images of fingerprints in police databases. When an investigation turns up sets of prints that need to be identified, the computer will search those databases and pick out the closest matches for experts to study. (Before computers, investigators

Improving the Image

Special programs enable computers to perform many crime fighting tasks, such as enhancing, or improving the quality of, images. Computer experts can improve a poor-quality video or photograph so that a person's face is recognizable or a license plate can be read clearly. Other experts use computer programs to complete a partial fingerprint, to provide a three-dimensional view of a two-dimensional image, or to reconstruct a sequence of events such as a car crash. Those operations may not always produce evidence acceptable in court, but they can help identify suspects or give the police important leads to follow.

had to look through books containing thousands of images of fingerprints to try to find a match.) Computers can also be programmed to search databases for matches of guns, cartridges and bullets, hairs, fibers, paint chips, and many other types of physical evidence.

Computers can perform those searches in minutes, while similar operations would take humans hundreds, perhaps thousands, of hours. A large computer database can hold massive amounts of information in which important details might be missed. In the case of a British serial killer nicknamed the "Yorkshire Ripper," investigators piled up an unmanageable mass of documents. There was so much information that no one spotted the fact that a man named Peter William Sutcliffe had been interviewed nine times in different places. Today, a quick database check would instantly highlight that suspicious fact.

Peter William Sutcliffe, the "Yorkshire Ripper," leaves court under heavy police guard. Sutcliffe was convicted of killing 13 women in the United Kingdom between 1975 and 1980.

The details of a suspect are displayed on a police computer. Computer technology gives investigators instant access to a vast amount of information.

 PROS: COMPUTER TECHNOLOGY

Computer technology has made crime fighting more efficient, enabling investigators to identify suspects and gather evidence more quickly than in the past. More efficient policing may help catch criminals before they can commit further crimes, increasing confidence in public safety.

CONS: COMPUTER TECHNOLOGY

Police staff are often in short supply. Resources spent on computers might be better spent on employing more officers to patrol the streets. People increasingly rely on databases, but those are not foolproof. In 2002, for instance, a school caretaker in Cambridgeshire, United Kingdom, killed two students. The man had passed a background check before he was hired. It failed to show that he had been investigated by child protection agencies and was once arrested for burglary.

Global Computers

The information society is global. Computers in nearly every country send information to one another. Law enforcement agencies of different nations regularly exchange information with one another and with the international police agency, Interpol. The United States and the European Union already share much data relevant to crime and terrorism, and plans are in place to link the databases of the 27 member countries of the European Union.

Most democracies protect the privacy of innocent people by limiting the information about them that can be stored in a database. Database information is usually confined to facts about people who have committed crimes or who have had contact with law enforcement. However, police agencies are currently in favor of building databases that will include facts about all citizens, whether they have committed crimes or not.

Computers and Law Enforcement

VIEWPOINT

In 2006, a computer and security expert wrote about the importance of using computers to help to solve crimes:

"Computer forensics and digital investigations have become an integral part of police work in the new millennium. Computers are now as much a part of the modern law enforcement officer's daily routine as the baton, side arm, two-way radio, or handcuffs."

(Gary C. Kessler, Associate Professor of Digital Information Management at Champlain College, Burlington, Vermont)

A police officer uses a handheld computer to access information on a central database while out on patrol.

PROS: DATABASES

Databases help police solve crimes more efficiently. The bigger the database, the more effectively it can be used. (If a database contains only records of known criminals, for instance, first-time offenders may escape justice because they will not appear in the database.) Information exchanged between national databases has already proved useful in catching criminals who have fled to other countries.

CONS: DATABASES

People are reluctant to give the government more power over their lives. They fear, sometimes rightly, that such power will be abused. In 2008, an investigation revealed that police in Sada, Spain, had created an illegal database of personal details and photographs for political use, not for fighting crime. Human errors have already shown that databases are far from secure. In 2007, about 79 million records containing personal information were lost or stolen from databases in the United States. Worldwide, that figure was about 162 million.

Computer Crime

Computers can aid in law enforcement, but criminals can also benefit from them. A computer can be used to plan a robbery or design false documents that look incredibly convincing. Criminals can also exploit the interconnectedness of the world's computer networks. That maximizes a criminal's ability to access and send information, but it has its downsides. Terrorists in different countries can use the Internet to make contact and organize their activities. They can even learn how to make a bomb by studying the information available online.

Con artists and terrorists also operate online, usually by taking false identities. They persuade people to part with money in return for nonexistent goods or bogus business opportunities. Even more sinister cases have involved adults entering young people's online chat rooms. Those adults pretend to be young people, hoping to find victims they can abuse.

Another serious criminal activity involves using a computer to break into other people's computers or private networks. That is called hacking. Computer hackers search for personal information such as names, Social Security numbers, and bank account and credit card information. Criminals can use those facts to steal their victims' money or buy goods in their name. That crime, known as identity theft, can be hard to investigate. Victims may find it difficult to prove that they were not the people who withdrew the money or incurred the debts.

Credit cards are often used to make online purchases. Credit card numbers and other details, sent over the Internet, can be exploited by criminals.

Invisible Evidence

Criminals sometimes believe they can cover their tracks by deleting computer files or e-mails that could be used as evidence against them. They are often wrong. When a file is deleted, its title is erased and new material can be written over its contents. But until the overwriting is done, the contents still exist and a police expert can recover them. Even overwriting may not wipe out an entire file, since computers often break up large files and store them in different places. If even small parts of an incriminating file survive, they may provide useful evidence.

British hacker Gary McKinnon meets the press in London in 2009. McKinnon hacked into many U.S. military sites. He claimed that he was searching for evidence of UFOs. U.S. authorities have accused him of sabotage and want to put him on trial in the United States.

Hackers and Viruses

Not all people who hack into computer systems are thieves. Some hackers are skillful computer enthusiasts who operate in groups. They may want to publicize their opinions or may get a thrill from exposing weaknesses in computer networks. High-profile victims have included the U.S. Department of Defense and the U.S. space agency, NASA. Hackers may just alter an organization's home page as a prank or may do more serious damage by altering or deleting important information.

The most malicious and dangerous computer crime is to create and release a computer virus. A virus is a program that spreads from computer to computer, infecting entire networks. Most often, the virus disables or damages the computer's operating system, and sometimes data, causing problems that may cost millions, even billions, of dollars to correct or eliminate.

Government agencies patrol the Internet, on the watch for fraudulent sites and terrorist communications. However, there is a strong tradition of respecting privacy in democracies. That means that law enforcement has only limited access to communications such as e-mails unless very serious crimes are suspected.

Tracing computer criminals is difficult, since many of them are skillful at concealing their physical addresses. As the Internet is worldwide, criminals may live far from the scenes of their crimes. Computer users have to be vigilant in identifying malicious activities. Organizations can protect themselves against hackers with the help of security companies and intrusion detection systems. Alert computer users watch for viruses, do not open unusual e-mails, update systems regularly, and use protective measures, such as firewalls and antivirus software. Combating hacking is an ongoing battle as both sides devise new, high-tech weapons.

 PROS: POLICING THE INTERNET

The Internet has become a vital means of communicating, both for business and personal use. Protecting computer systems against terrorists, hackers, and other criminals remains a high priority.

 CONS: POLICING THE INTERNET

The Internet is uniquely open and uncensored. It will stay that way only if there are strict limits on governments' abilities to regulate it.

VIEWPOINT

Internet Crime

In 2006, Robert S. Mueller, III, Director of the U.S. Federal Bureau of Investigation (FBI), discussed the difficulty of tackling Internet crime:

"Cyber [computer-related] crime is a growing threat. Today, terrorists coordinate their plans cloaked in the anonymity of the Internet, as do violent sexual predators prowling chat rooms .... All too often, we find that before we can catch these offenders, Internet service providers have unwittingly deleted the very records that would help us identify these offenders and protect future victims. We must find a balance between the legitimate need for privacy and law enforcement's clear need for access."

CHAPTER 3

Watching and Listening

People in modern societies are very mobile. They are free to decide what they want to do and where they want to go. Criminals also enjoy those freedoms. Law enforcers can, however, use a range of modern technologies to overhear, watch, and track the movement of suspected criminals. Those activities are described as surveillance or, when they involve listening to conversations, eavesdropping.

Eavesdropping

The police can listen in on private conversations by placing a wiretap on a suspect's telephone line. Wiretapping is an old technology, dating back to the 1890s. When someone answers the phone, the line becomes an electric circuit. It is a fairly simple operation to plug a listening device into the circuit. Today, criminals communicate via cell phones, but the police can also tap cell phones and, through them, track suspects as they move from place to place.

Law enforcement agencies can listen to conversations with the help of a bug — a tiny microphone that can be hidden in a room. The bug transmits everything that is said via radio waves to police officers stationed nearby. Bugs have been used in spying operations for a long time, but modern versions are more effective than ever. Thanks to recent

Alarming Technologies

Most stores and organizations, and many homes, have electronic alarm systems to protect them from burglars. The wide variety of devices includes wired and wireless alarms. Some merely ring out or light up an area around a house. Others are linked to police stations or security centers, notifying them of an unauthorized entry. Unfortunately, more than 92 percent of alarms are activated by failures in the equipment or mistakes made by users. As a result, neighbors, passersby, and even police are often slow to take alarms seriously. However, evidence shows that places with alarm systems have a much reduced risk of being entered illegally.

advancements in miniaturization, they are so tiny that they are almost impossible to detect.

To plant a bug in a room where suspects live or meet, a police officer must enter it while no one is there. That operation may risk alerting suspected criminals. Other devices can pick up conversations on the street more than 300 feet (91 meters) away without any approach by an officer. Another option is to "wire" an undercover officer with a hidden microphone. That officer will talk with criminals, hoping to lead them to reveal their plans or make statements that reveal their guilt.

A surveillance expert displays a microphone concealed inside a small lighter. That mic could be used for many purposes, including spying on private meetings where illegal activities are discussed.

All of those forms of eavesdropping interfere with people's privacy. Countries take different views of that problem. In most democracies, the police need to convince a court of law that the suspect is involved in a serious matter before they are permitted to eavesdrop.

 PROS: EAVESDROPPING

Bugs and similar electronic devices can monitor criminal activity without risking the lives of police officers. The information they provide may prevent some crimes and often leads to arrests of some criminals and convictions of others.

CONS: EAVESDROPPING

Like the monitoring of e-mails, eavesdropping is very intrusive. In effect, government agents invade people's homes, causing outrage when the victims are found innocent of any crime. One of the worst features of eavesdropping technology is that it can also be used by unofficial individuals or organizations, such as con artists, identity thieves, businesses spying on rival companies, or criminals seeking opportunities for theft or blackmail.

Seeing Is Believing

In recent years, the growth of visual surveillance has been spectacular. Its most common form is closed-circuit television (CCTV). Basically, CCTV consists of one or more video cameras that transmit a signal to a chosen location where the moving images can be viewed on monitors. For security people watching those monitors, it is like viewing television. But the closed circuit means that no outsider can watch those monitors. Increasingly, CCTV is also equipped to record sound.

The police install CCTV cameras in public places and buildings. Big institutions, shops, and individuals install private CCTV in many places, including shopping centers, hospitals, car parks, and homes. Those cameras provide evidence of shoplifting, vandalism, burglary, and more serious crimes, such as assault. To monitor the area, security personnel are stationed in front of various screens that show different parts of a building or park. In other cases, no one watches all the time, but officers can view recorded tapes later if a serious incident has occurred.

VIEWPOINT

Good or Bad?

The benefits of surveillance are praised by some people and questioned by others:

"It is the clear benefits of CCTV in fighting crime — from terrorism down to antisocial behavior — which have led to its increased use by the police and transportation and local authorities — and also by shops and businesses."

(Gordon Brown, Prime Minister of the United Kingdom)

"Once [surveillance] information is collected, it will be misused, lost, and stolen. It will be filled with errors. The problems and insecurities that come from living in a surveillance society more than outweigh any crime-fighting (and terrorist-fighting) advantages."

(Bruce Schneier, U.S. security expert and author)

Surveillance cameras have become a familiar sight in many countries. They are designed to protect property and record criminal behavior.

Large numbers of CCTV cameras operate in major cities all over the world. Since the 1990s, the United Kingdom has made a particularly big investment in the technology. It has installed many more cameras, in proportion to population numbers, than the United States. Some British citizens are watched on CCTV hundreds of times a day. In 2008, a British train company even decided to equip inspectors with small CCTV cameras, worn on their helmets. Critics have pointed out that crime statistics have not fallen significantly as a result of the large-scale and very expensive installation of CCTV systems. On the other hand, CCTV has proved valuable on some important occasions. In 1993, a child named James Bulger went missing in a shopping center in Merseyside, United Kingdom. CCTV footage showed him leaving the center with two boys. Instead of looking for adult kidnappers, the police followed the evidence and caught the boys, who had murdered the child. CCTV also helped to trace terrorists who attacked the London subway and a bus in 2005.

The Surveillance Camera Players held up signs in Times Square in New York City in 2006 to advertise a play about the uselessness of CCTV cameras as a tool for reducing crime.

PROS: CLOSED-CIRCUIT TELEVSION

The presence of surveillance equipment, such as CCTV, makes it far more likely that criminals will be brought to justice. Videotaped images, unlike recorded voices, offer evidence that is hard to dispute. Clear CCTV evidence often persuades criminals to confess, saving courts time and money. In the long run, successful surveillance may make would-be criminals and vandals less inclined to wrongdoing. Either way, society gains in security.

CONS: CLOSED-CIRCUIT TELEVISION

The cost of large-scale CCTV surveillance, such as in the United Kingdom, is huge. Crime rates have hardly been reduced, and criminals have found ways to conceal their identities by wearing hoods or masks. CCTV, like eavesdropping, tends to be unpopular. People dislike the idea that the authorities know everything they do or say.

Speed Cameras

Closed-circuit television networks on national highway systems monitor drivers and the shipment of freight. Huge amounts of freight, or goods, are transported every day, and millions of people drive on roads for business and pleasure. Efforts to police that huge and complicated traffic network rely heavily on advanced surveillance systems.

Many people drive too fast or are reckless in other ways, such as running red lights or driving after drinking alcohol. Surveillance technology is used to persuade motorists to obey the law. In some places where accidents are common, electronic road signs remind motorists of the speed limit and warn them if they are driving too fast. However, technology is more often employed to identify and penalize offenders, such as to capture images of toll evaders.

VIEWPOINT

Case Proved?

"The presence of safety cameras has been proven, time and again, to reduce speeding and save lives and does play a major part in reducing collisions."

(Chief Inspector Brian Kee, Northern Ireland Road Policing Department, 2007)

The most widely used instruments are speed cameras. They photograph passing vehicles and calculate the speed at which they are traveling. The registration on the number plate is checked against data stored in a central computer. That identifies the vehicle's owner, who will be held responsible for disobeying any laws. However, the real point of installing speed cameras is to encourage drivers not to break the law and endanger lives. The speed camera is also a weapon against crime. If the database lists a vehicle caught on camera as stolen, or as having been used during a crime, the police will act at once to pursue and stop it.

Many drivers consult online maps to locate the speed cameras on their intended routes, so those cameras can be avoided. In response, manufacturers have developed mobile speed camera units, handheld cameras that police officers can use in their vehicles to pursue criminal activities wherever they take place. The positions of those cameras are not fixed, so drivers cannot anticipate them. Many similar cameras monitor other types of activity, including the way drivers behave at red lights, pedestrian crossings, construction zones, and near schools. Cameras are also installed at tollbooths to ensure that drivers pay tolls.

Crafty Cameras

Most speed cameras operate in a fixed position and take flash photographs. To avoid dazzling the oncoming driver, the camera photographs the rear of the vehicle, including the license plate. Because there is no picture of the driver, the owner may claim not to have been driving at the time. Many drivers know the locations of speed cameras and break the speed limit except when they are in sight of a camera. More recent technology tackles those problems. Cameras photograph vehicles from the front using infrared light, which is invisible to the human eye. Sensors in the road can calculate the vehicle's speed over a measured distance, rather than at one single moment.

Safety First

VIEWPOINT

In 2009, Maryland Senator James N. Robey, a former police chief, said why he had proposed that the state install more speed cameras:

"It's about safety. We can't put police officers everywhere, but we have the technology to reduce speed. We should use it."

A police officer stands by a radar gun that records the speeds of passing vehicles. People who drive over the speed limit will be caught and punished.

 PROS: SPEED CAMERAS

In countries where millions of vehicles use the roads, reducing the number of deaths and injuries is obviously beneficial to society. Equipment such as speed cameras also helps control crimes, such as car theft.

 CONS: SPEED CAMERAS

Many motorists resent speed cameras. They feel they are treated as criminals for breaking minor laws, such as driving just a mile or two over the speed limit. Some motorists have voiced their suspicion that authorities use speed cameras to make money by issuing an increasing number of speeding tickets rather than to save lives.

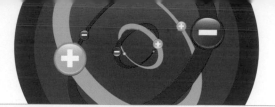

CHAPTER 4

Global Threats

In recent years, issues of security and surveillance have become increasingly important because of the threats presented by terrorism. Motivated by extreme political or religious beliefs, terrorists launch violent attacks on people and places. Their targets are often nonmilitary, and the attacks generally cost innocent lives. Terrorism is not new, but in the 21st century the threat of terrorism has become alarmingly serious.

On September 11, 2001, now widely known as 9/11, members of the terrorist group al-Qaeda hijacked four planes and crashed two of them

Memorial lights shine over the Hudson River in New York City, marking where the twin towers of the World Trade Center stood until a devastating terrorist attack destroyed them in September 2001.

into the twin towers of the World Trade Center in New York City. Nearly 3,000 people were killed and the towers were totally destroyed. Other violent incidents in Bali, Indonesia, and Moscow in 2002, in Madrid in 2004, in London in 2005, and in Mumbai, India, in 2008, confirmed that terrorism had become more destructive and globalized than ever before.

Fighting Terrorism

Terrorism is among the most difficult crimes for police and security forces to prevent. Terrorists may strike anywhere and many of them are prepared to take part in suicide missions, giving up their lives in order to kill others. Security forces react by trying to identify and monitor likely suspects. If possible, they use informers or Federal Bureau of Intelligence (FBI) agents to learn what terrorist groups are planning. Those agents can also monitor e-mails, computer web sites, and phone conversations.

Electronic Passports

Passports are government-issued documents that identify people and allow them to travel between countries. Biometric passports contain an additional feature, a computer microchip with images of the holder and details about him or her. That type of passport is more difficult to forge or to tamper with than a conventional passport. In 2008, a new facial recognition system was given a trial at Manchester Airport in the United Kingdom. Holders of biometric passports were allowed through unstaffed "smart gates" that had sensors that could scan the microchip images and their data. If the information corresponded with that on the airport database, the passport holder passed through rapidly. The system is expected to save time and money.

Many public places are protected by CCTV. The officers who monitor the CCTV screens must remain alert for anything that appears to be out of the ordinary. Entry to some buildings, such as business or government offices, is highly restricted. Many of those buildings have high-tech identification (ID) systems. People authorized to enter the building have ID cards, called "smart cards," that contain a computer microchip. Millions of people also have electronic or biometric passports, which function in the same way. Many European countries have taken electronic identification even further, issuing compulsory ID cards to all their citizens.

PROS: ANTITERRORISM MEASURES

Large-scale security measures make life safer and give people confidence to go on leading normal lives, despite the ongoing threat of terrorism.

 CONS: ANTITERRORISM MEASURES

Society could easily feel like a police-state, with constant ID checks and searches. Some people feel that citizens are already subject to too much surveillence. For example, the police presence has been increased in many countries to combat terrorism. Such increased presence, however, may limit personal freedom and could make it easier for corrupt police officers to abuse their authority.

Travelers' Troubles

Airports and railway stations, which are often thronged with travelers, are obvious targets for terrorism. Since 9/11, airport security has made it more difficult for a terrorist to board a plane, and more difficult still to bring weapons or bombs on board. At airports, passengers must allow their belts, shoes, and hand luggage to be inspected by security officers. (The potential threat from shoes was only realized when British terrorist Richard Reid was caught on a U.S. airliner with explosives in his sneakers.) Then passengers pass through an arched metal detector. If the detector sounds a warning signal, the passenger will probably be searched. That can be done by using a backscatter X-ray machine, which has

A "See-Through" Machine

The backscatter X-ray is a new imaging system that has recently been introduced at major U.S. airports. Standard X-rays pass through objects, producing images that are detailed enough for medical purposes. But for surveillance, such images can be blurry and confusing. The backscatter X-ray sends high-energy rays that scatter over the target, rather than passing through it. As a result, the images it produces are more three-dimensional and well-defined. As the machine passes over a vehicle, it reveals the presence of any concealed drugs, weapons, or people. When directed at a person, backscatter X-ray machines show the subject unclothed, revealing any hidden weapons or devices.

caused controversy because it produces images that show its subjects as though they are naked. However, some people argue that the machine is preferable to manual "pat-down" hand searches. Airport and airline staff must go through similar procedures. Only then are passengers and staff allowed into areas with access to runways and planes.

A backscatter X-ray machine reveals the presence of illegal immigrants inside a vehicle bringing bananas from Mexico into the United States.

 PROS: SECURITY CHECKS

Unchecked terrorism could inflict far more damage on society than anything that ordinary criminals can do. For that reason, people realize the importance of security measures. They support those measures even when they cause inconvenience or violate personal privacy.

 CONS: SECURITY CHECKS

Heavy security can cause delays and congestion at airports, crowding that slows the system and disrupts schedules. Those delays can inflict serious economic damage on transportation, tourism, and commerce. There are also fears that governments will use anti-terrorism laws and security measures to limit the freedoms and privacy of their citizens.

Blocking the Blast

Even the tightest security may fail to prevent a terrorist attack. There have been many examples of suicide bombers driving vehicles filled with explosives into high-security areas such as military barracks. Using that tactic, terrorists have taken many lives, especially at U.S. sites throughout the world. To counter those threats, crash-proof barrier systems have been developed. One example is the DSC 501, a pop-up barrier that

A soldier passes a burned-out vehicle following a 2008 car bomb assault on the U.S. Embassy in Yemen. Security barriers helped to minimize the effects of the attack.

activates automatically if it senses a vehicle driving toward it at high speed. It can stop a 7-ton (6.4-metric ton) truck traveling at 50 miles per hour (80 kilometers per hour) and remain operational after several attacks.

Public places are also vulnerable. For example, a terrorist may be able to plant a bomb in a crowded place without being spotted on CCTV. However, a small device, currently being tested at British airports and railway stations, may provide the answer. It contains a laser that can scan a crowd and identify people who have been handling explosives. The device detects traces of explosive residue on people or their belongings.

The possibility that terrorists might acquire nuclear devices, or the materials needed to make them, has also led to the development of new equipment. In 2005, specialist manufacturers created the Miniature Integrated Nuclear Detection System (MINDS), which can scan vehicles, vessels, and luggage. That system can detect the radiation emitted by the presence of nuclear material.

Challenging Terrorism

VIEWPOINT

On February 4, 2008, 12 million people in 190 cities joined protests against the Colombian terrorist group FARC. The global protests were organized entirely online. James K. Glassman, U.S. Under Secretary for Public Diplomacy and Public Affairs, praised the effort:

"Around the world, young people are using the Internet to push back against violence in a new way, using social networking … basically to share information. And that is something that al-Qaeda and the violent extremist groups cannot stand. We think the technology that exists today is on our side; it's not on the extremists' side."

Security forces regularly check for bombs. They use high-tech devices including sensors for locating explosives placed underneath cars. But bomb-sniffing dogs, trained to identify the chemicals used in explosives, also play an important role. If there is any evidence that someone has planted a bomb, the area will immediately be cleared of people, and security officers will begin new and urgent searches.

Finding a Bomb

If a bomb is discovered, a bomb disposal team will attempt to prevent it from exploding, or ensure that the damage caused by the explosion is contained. Today, bomb disposal experts seldom need to risk their lives by dismantling explosives. A mobile robot is sent to the scene and the experts control its operation from a safe distance. Even if the robot succeeds, the officers in charge take no chances. The next step is to destroy the bomb with a controlled explosion. That is an explosion that minimizes the risk and damage involved. For example, officers place an explosive device next to the suspected bomb. They then case both objects in protective steel or wrap them in heavy protective material before blowing them up.

Humans keep their distance while a Nepalese Army bomb disposal robot removes a suspicious package left on a parked motorcycle in Tibet, a region in the People's Republic of China. The use of robots for the dangerous job of bomb disposal has saved many lives.

Investigating Disaster

Sometimes, in spite of all precautions, terrorists launch successful attacks. In similar scenarios, disasters occur that may or may not be accidental, such as airliner crashes. The people who investigate those disasters will draw upon the resources of forensic science and technology. In land-based cases, CCTV and witness statements will help investigators establish what happened and who was responsible. Incidents in the air present more difficulties, since there are often no survivors or witnesses. In 1988, Pan Am flight 103 exploded over Lockerbie, Scotland. Investigators had to comb through millions of pieces of debris to discover what triggered the explosion. After months of research, they concluded that the plane was brought down by a terrorist attack. In other cases, the aircraft's flight data recorder, or black box, may survive to shed light on an otherwise mysterious and tragic event.

The Black Box

Commercial and military aircraft carry a flight data recorder (FDR), commonly known as a black box. The "black" box is usually orange to make it easier to find after a crash. It is stowed in the aircraft's tail to protect it from a frontal crash. The black box is designed to withstand fire, water, and intense shocks. It records all the readings from the instruments in the cockpit. When first used in the 1950s, the FDR also recorded what pilots said. Today, a separate voice recorder in the cockpit usually does that.

 PROS: MEASURES TAKEN TO FIGHT TERRORISM

Terrorist attacks can lead to many deaths and are often felt as attacks on a country's or a people's entire way of life. Catching terrorists and preventing terrorist attacks are vital operations that most people support, even if tighter security measures reduce their civil liberties.

 CONS: MEASURES TAKEN TO FIGHT TERRORISM

Fears of terrorism have led governments in many countries to extend far greater powers to law enforcement agencies. The ability of police to stop and search individuals, for example, or to monitor their e-mails, may seriously interfere with civil liberties, such as the right to privacy.

CHAPTER 5

Questions of Identity

In a criminal case, investigators need to know the identities of the people involved. Without the names of suspects, victims, or witnesses, police find it hard to build a solid case or secure a conviction.

Whose Body Is It?

Most people carry documents or cards that identify them. Murder victims are most often killed by someone they know, often a spouse or family member. Police usually begin their investigation by interviewing the victim's family and friends, but if the victim is unknown, police have few leads to follow. For that reason, killers may go to great lengths to conceal their victims' identities. A murderer may remove all personal items from the scene. Some may even chop off the victim's hands or head to make him or her harder to identify. War criminals also try to hide evidence of genocide by burying bodies in mass graves.

When the body of an unknown person is found, the pathologist's examination will provide some clues to the corpse's identity. If certain parts of the skeleton survive, the pathologist will be able to learn the victim's gender and give accurate estimates of age, height, and other physical characteristics. Less complete remains may also yield information. Experts can make X-ray images of a corpse's teeth, hoping to find a match to an individual in a dental identification database.

If the remains are recognizable, the police may get results by circulating a description. If the corpse is badly mutilated or decayed, a forensic sculptor may be able to restore the victim's appearance with the help of advanced facial reconstruction techniques. The sculptor makes a cast of the skull to create an identical copy of it, then covers it with clay, modeling it to create a lifelike head. Similar results are achieved by scanning the information into a computer. Experts disagree as to whether better results are obtained by the computer's precision or the artist's talent.

Reconstructing a Face

A forensic sculptor works on a cast that is a copy of the victim's skull. Anatomists can predict, with accuracy, the thickness of the tissue — the flesh and skin — that covers the skull. Armed with that knowledge, the artist inserts pegs of different lengths into about 30 key points on the skull. Those lengths represent different thicknesses of tissue. The artist uses strips of clay to build up the clay to the right thickness. When glass eyes are inserted, the surface is painted, and details such as eyebrows and hair are added, the result is often very lifelike.

A forensic sculptor models clay over the cast of a victim's skull. Once a recreation of the person's facial appearance is completed, police may be able to more easily identify the victim.

Where Is the Body?

Sometimes police officers are faced with not only identifying a body, but also trying to find one. People go missing for all sorts of reasons. Some choose to disappear and start a new life, while others vanish in suspicious circumstances. When that happens, the police will investigate. But it is difficult for them to make a case for murder unless they can find a body.

Most murderers bury or abandon the bodies of their victims near the crime scenes. In many cases, a line search is all that is needed to locate those victims. To conduct a line search, police officers stand shoulder to shoulder in a long line and walk slowly forward, looking for any scrap of evidence on the ground. A plane or helicopter may also be used to scan for any unusual features, such as recently disturbed soil.

These Labrador dogs are being trained by handlers to search for the remains of dead bodies. Dogs have a very powerful sense of smell, which makes them useful in many types of police work.

The task of locating hidden bodies or graves is hardest when the search area is large or wild, and enough time has passed to cover up any signs of digging. Then even large-scale searches may not succeed. Between 1963 and 1965, Ian Brady and Myra Hindley committed some of the United Kingdom's most notorious crimes, murdering children and burying them on the rolling open grassland of the moors near Manchester. The body of one of their five known victims was discovered only in 1987, and the body of another victim is still missing.

Scientific Searches

Modern science and technology can help find missing bodies. NecroSearch International, for example, is a U.S.-based organization that brings together volunteer scientists and experts from a number of fields to help to locate hidden graves. Geophysics experts try to find graves by using remote sensing methods to spot unusual patterns in the soil without disturbing the evidence. Remote-sensing devices include ground-penetrating radar (GPR), which sends out radio waves that are reflected by unusual objects buried beneath the soil. Thermal imaging and infrared light can identify underground heat spots that may represent the heat given off by decaying bodies. Sonar scans operate like GPR, but make use of sound waves. Sonar is particularly useful in underwater searches.

Experts in botany, the science of plants, may locate a grave site by noticing a place where the vegetation is different from that of a nearby area. The reason could be that a body is fertilizing the soil, or that disturbance of the ground has given new plants the opportunity to take hold.

Ancient Crime Scene

When police in northern Europe investigate bodies found in peat bogs, they often suspect foul play. But if a forensic archaeologist tests the remains, the results can be surprising. In 2005, for example, diggers discovered the body of a teenage girl who had died violently. However, archaeologists showed that the corpse was 2,700 years old, her body preserved by acids in the peat. Her age was established by carbon dating. Every living thing contains a fixed proportion of a radioactive material, carbon-14, which decays at a constant rate after death. Scientists can tell, from the amount of carbon-14 remaining, how long ago a person died. Like the teenager, other "bog people" who were killed in ancient times, perhaps as sacrifices, have been similarly preserved.

Who Did It?

After a crime is committed, the police often find it easy to name one or more suspects. Those are likely to be people with strong links to the crime scene or the victim, who may have motives, such as jealousy or greed. In other cases, such as attacks by a stranger, the criminal may prove harder to identify. There may be plenty of forensic evidence at the crime scene, but unless it can be matched to an individual on a database, it will be of little value.

In these circumstances, the police try to find people who have witnessed the crime or have noticed a person acting suspiciously in the area. Criminals such as rapists often attack repeatedly, so it is likely that, sooner or later, someone will see or hear something useful. The police will then be able to circulate a description of the suspect. If witness descriptions are reasonably detailed, the police will try to create and distribute a picture of the person. They know that people tend to recognize images more easily than verbal descriptions.

The image may take the form of a sketch by an artist, based on witness interviews. Another more flexible method is for the police to use an identikit. They can put together a number of identikits that fit varying witness statements or include disguises such as beards and glasses.

PROS: IDENTIKITS

Identikits and artist's sketches of suspects give better results than written descriptions because people are more likely to recognize individuals from pictures than from words. Indentikits of suspects can be published in newspapers and on television, improving the chances of catching them.

CONS: IDENTIKITS

Identikits and similar techniques are only as good as the witness statements on which they are based. Witnesses often have confused recollections of what they have seen and heard, so the use of identikits may lead to incorrect identifications and miscarriages of justice.

Identikits

The first identikit was the brainchild of a Los Angeles police officer named Hugh C. McDonald. Developed from 1959, the first pack consisted of 525 transparent sheets. Each sheet carried a drawing of a single facial feature. Witnesses chose an example of each feature from a selection. Police officers then stacked the sheets on top of one another. The assembled features created a single image of the suspect's face. In 1970, Jacques Penry introduced a new and expanded identikit system, the photo-FIT, in the United Kingdom. That system used photographs of individual features, presented as horizontal strips that could be fitted together like a jigsaw puzzle. Today, police use computer software versions of identikits.

A crime expert (*front*) helps a victim build a picture of a suspected criminal. Each horizontal strip shows a single facial feature. The victim chooses the features one by one to create an image of the suspect.

Profiling

When tracking an unidentified offender, the police may call in a criminal profiler to help. Profilers are experts who attempt to understand the personalities and behavior of criminals in order to solve crimes. The profilers' conclusions enable police to focus their efforts on specific types of people or particular places. Like identikits, profiling is only science-based, not an exact science, so it is not always successful.

Inside a Criminal's Mind

Profilers try to understand and predict criminals' behavior. This may be important for solving crimes that do not involve easily understood motives such as greed and revenge — for example, random gun attacks, rape, arson, or serial murders. Having studied similar crimes, profilers attempt to predict characteristics, such as the age, gender, and occupation of the criminal. The profiler is often an expert psychologist with insight into the criminal's mentality and motives. In kidnapping and hostage-taking incidents, successfully negotiating with the criminals may depend on knowing how they think and are likely to behave.

⊕ PROS: CRIMINAL PROFILING

Crimes committed by an unknown person or persons are particularly unnerving. Widely reported in the media, they undermine people's belief that they live in a safe society. Profilers can help police narrow the search for suspects. They can also help police inform the public about what kind of person they should avoid. Profilers also try to predict where the criminal is likely to strike next.

⊖ CONS: CRIMINAL PROFILING

Profiling is not always accurate and can lead police to make mistakes. For instance, profilers have observed that most serial killers are white males in their thirties. However, there have been female and African American serial killers too, and some have remained at large longer than necessary because they did not fit the standard profile. Critics also say that profiling is unfair because it targets entire groups of people, based on generalized characteristics, such as race and religion.

DNA Profiling

The greatest single advance in forensic identification has been DNA testing. Molecules of DNA (deoxyribonucleic acid) are present in almost every cell in the human body. DNA inside the nucleus at the core of a cell holds the instructions that determine what we look like and how our cells and bodies function. DNA molecules are vital and are often described as the building blocks of life.

DNA was discovered in the 19th-century, but it was only in 1953, thanks to researchers James Watson and Francis Crick, that scientists understood its structure. The DNA in most cells is in the form of a double helix — two twisting, interlinked strands, rather like a spiral ladder. Special sequences of DNA, called genes, appear at intervals on the ladder. Those determine all of an individual's physical characteristics.

DNA sequences are often called the building blocks of life because they contain the information and instructions that make us who we are. The twisting, ladder-like structure of DNA is called a double helix.

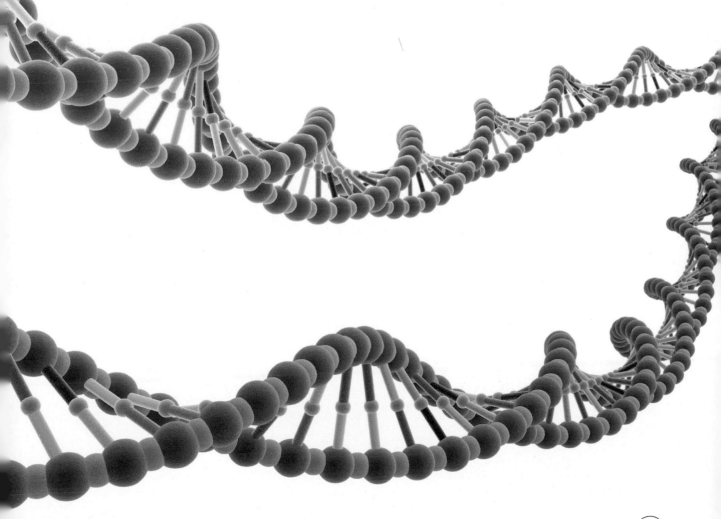

Using DNA as a means of identifying individuals was pioneered in 1985 by British biochemist Alec John Jeffreys, working at the University of Leicester in the United Kingdom. Surprisingly, DNA testing for identification does not rely on the crucial areas of the ladder that carry the genes, but on other, apparently less useful stretches that are sometimes described as "junk DNA". In those areas of the ladder, the rungs consist of short sequences of chemical combinations that are repeated. The number of times the sequence is repeated is varied and unpredictable. Ten to 15 different sequences, known as genetic markers, taken from a DNA sample will contain repeated combinations that are unique to an individual. Only identical twins or other close siblings will have the same, or very similar, genetic markers.

That means that an individual's DNA provides the most reliable kind of evidence to identify a person. Experts can extract DNA from tiny drops of blood, saliva, hair roots, and most other biological materials. Such evidence from a crime scene can be used to create a DNA profile. That profile can then be compared with samples taken from suspects or from DNA profiles stored in police databases. A positive match proves that the suspect was present at the scene of the crime. DNA comparisons may also eliminate nonmatching individuals from the investigation.

Processing DNA

The forensic team preserves any cells with DNA discovered at the crime scene. Later, police officers take samples from suspects by gently swabbing the insides of their cheeks. Back in the laboratory, technicians use chemicals to dissolve the cell walls and isolate the DNA. They cut it into segments and, if necessary, use a special technique to increase the amount. Then they pass an electric current through the DNA, which drives it through a tube and sorts it into bands. Fixed on to a nylon sheet, the DNA now resembles a barcode and can be compared with similarly coded samples. Different processing methods can record the DNA as number sets that are suitable for use in computer databases.

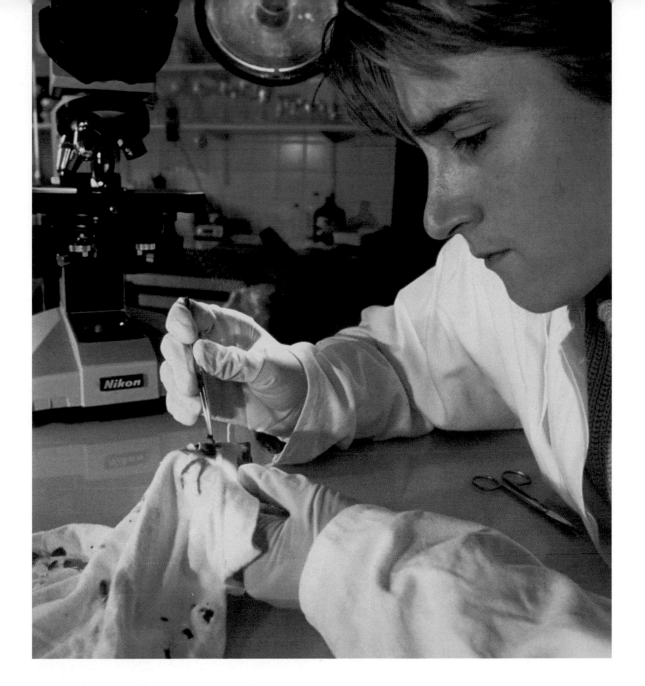

Revisiting Old Cases

DNA testing can be applied to old cases as long as human remains, or samples taken at the time, are available. One of the triumphs of DNA testing has been to prove the innocence of individuals who were wrongly convicted of crimes. In 2003, convicted murderer Rudolph Holton was released from prison in Florida after serving 16 years on death row, awaiting execution if his appeals failed. New testing of DNA evidence had proved his innocence. By 2009, DNA testing had overturned the convictions of 233 people in the United States alone.

A forensic scientist removes a fragment of material from a blood-soaked garment found at a crime scene. That fabric will provide a blood sample from which a DNA profile will be constructed.

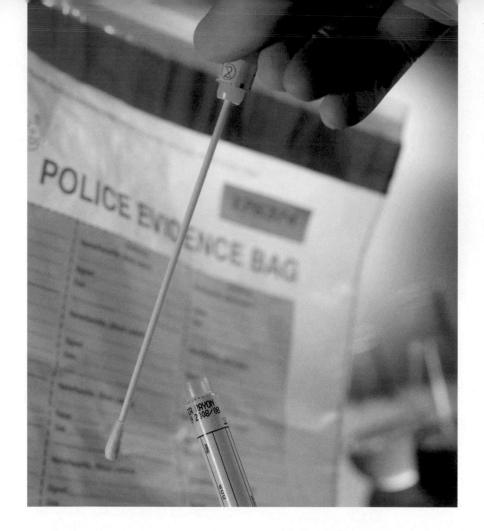

This swab sample carries saliva taken from a suspect, witness, or victim. It will be placed in a container that will prevent it from being contaminated. A DNA profile may be obtained from that sample.

DNA can also establish whether two people are related. In one famous case, bones were discovered that were believed to be those of Russian emperor, Tsar Nicholas II and his family, who were shot by revolutionaries in 1918. DNA was extracted from the bones and compared with a sample given by a relation of the Russian royal family, the Duke of Edinburgh, husband of Britain's Queen Elizabeth II. DNA analysis found a relationship between the samples and identified the bones beyond any serious doubt.

DNA Success

VIEWPOINT

Mike Rann, Premier of South Australia, wrote about DNA testing in 2004:

"[The government's] expansion of DNA testing has created one of South Australia's greatest crime fighting advancements since fingerprinting .... The expansion of DNA testing will ultimately help reduce the amount of time spent on investigations and in the courts, and most importantly it makes criminals responsible for their actions. Offenders now have the greatest chance of getting caught and they should consider themselves warned."

DNA Databases

Governments and police officials are interested in expanding DNA databases. The United States has the world's largest government database, containing more than 5 million profiles. Laws passed in 2004 and 2005 gave the U.S. government expanded powers to collect and store an increasing number of samples. The U.K.'s database of more than 4 million samples is even bigger in proportion to its population. However, in 2008, the European Court of Justice ruled that the United Kingdom would have to destroy samples from people who had been charged with a crime but not convicted. Unless reversed, that ruling meant that there would be limits on the expansion of DNA databases in the European Union.

 PROS: DNA TESTING

Forensic evidence often needs to be interpreted by an expert who may be swayed by a conscious or unconscious bias. But DNA testing is entirely science-based. Its lack of bias is shown by the fact that it has overturned convictions as well as secured them. Larger and fuller databases will make DNA testing an even more effective crime-fighting tool.

 CONS: DNA TESTING

DNA evidence is bound to influence judges and juries. It may also mislead them. DNA evidence may prove that a person was present at a crime scene, but will not necessarily prove that person committed the crime. Since DNA profiles of siblings are extremely similar and identical twins are a match, a DNA profile may not always be certain proof of an individual's identity. In addition, there is always the possibility that DNA evidence will become contaminated, for example, if a police officer carries a trace of DNA from a crime scene and then handles something belonging to a suspect. That DNA could then provide a false link between the crime scene and suspect, possibly leading to the conviction of an innocent person. For that reason, British law does not allow a conviction to be based on DNA evidence alone.

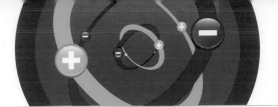

CHAPTER 6

In the Line of Duty

In many ways, law enforcement has not changed over the centuries. Police officers still have to maintain order. They pursue fleeing suspects, who may be armed and dangerous, and restrain and arrest them. However, science and technology have helped to make police work safer and more effective.

Terrorist threats have meant that British police carry arms much more often than in the past. Here, an officer guards a London railway station.

New Weapons

Police officers often have to meet violence with violence. In the United States and many other countries, police carry firearms. British police units are famous for being unarmed, but the rise in gun violence and terrorism has meant that officers of the Specialist Firearms Command (CO19) carry firearms openly. Modern technology has greatly improved police officers' chances of surviving encounters with armed criminals, for example, by equipping them with body armor that is bulletproof and stab-resistant.

Most police officers try not to fire their weapons even when they are faced with a possibly violent individual. Such a person may be upset or mentally disturbed rather than knowingly breaking the law.

In recent years, technology has offered police a number of nonlethal alternatives. The best-known is the Taser, a device that delivers an electric shock that temporarily disables its victim. Other nonlethal devices achieve a similar effect by delivering a violent blow to the targeted person. Police can also fire bullet-like plastic pellets, technically known as attenuated energy projectiles (AEPs), at the belt-buckle area of the target's body. As an additional safety feature, the nose of the pellet is designed to collapse if it hits a hard area of the body, such as the skull, so that it is less harmful.

The use of such nonlethal devices will frequently avoid a clash that could end in the death of suspects, police officers, or innocent bystanders. Experts currently disagree about the potential dangers of the devices. For instance, since the start of their use in 2001, approximately 334 deaths have been attributed to Tasers in the United States, according to Amnesty International.

How Tasers Work

A Taser is easy to operate and control. A police officer attaches a cartridge to the device. It is fired by a mechanism that breaks open a cylinder of compressed gas. The cartridge contains two electrically charged barbs, each trailing a conductive wire. The barbs attach to the target's skin or clothing like fishhooks, and an electric current is sent down the wires. The five-second shock temporarily disables the suspect, and the police are able to make an arrest without resistance.

Powerful jets from water cannons hit demonstrators in Paris, France, during a day of antigovernment protests in 2006. Water cannons are highly effective in riot control, but they can also be used to put down legitimate forms of legal protest.

Avoiding lethal violence is extremely important when the police face a crowd that threatens to become violent or begin a riot. Forces in many parts of the world use water cannons, mounted on armored vehicles, to discourage crowds. The cannons fire jets of water that hit people hard, driving them back. Other weapons include AEPs and chemical devices such as OC spray (pepper spray) and CS gas (tear gas), both of which powerfully irritate the eyes, nose, and throat. However, the use of nonlethal weapons can result in deaths. For instance, police in Massachusetts fired pepper spray to break up a crowd in 2004. One of the pepper spray pellets entered the eye of a 21-year-old college student and killed her. That incident led some U.S. police departments to stop using certain nonlethal weapons.

Nonlethal Weapons

VIEWPOINT

Many U.S. states are studying the effectiveness of nonlethal weapons, with a view to introduce them to more police departments. Still, many people disagree about how useful they are:

"For the first time in history, we are starting to gain technologies that will provide us the ability to use less-lethal force in resolving what have historically been lethal situations."

Charles "Sid" Heal, Retired Captain of the Los Angeles County Sheriff's Department, Los Angeles, California

"When you're dealing with real-life bullets, it makes no sense to come back with nonlethal weapons."

Major Don Woodruff, Duluth Police Department, Duluth, Georgia

PROS: NONLETHAL WEAPONS

Nonlethal weapons give police more options, particularly when dealing with someone who is mentally disturbed or in situations where firing a gun could pose a threat to innocent bystanders. The ability of police to control crowds and prevent riots makes societies more secure.

 CONS: NONLETHAL WEAPONS

Some supposedly nonlethal weapons may be more dangerous than their users believe. In the United States and Canada, a number of deaths have been linked to the use, or abuse, of Tasers. Officers may be tempted to treat weapons such as Tasers as an easy solution — for example, firing them rather than taking time to persuade a disturbed individual to cooperate. Rogue officers could use Tasers to bully or hurt innocent people. Tasers, water cannons, and CS gas can be, and in some countries have been, used to put down lawful demonstrations against heads of state, politicians, and their policies.

Chasing Criminals

Some of the most dangerous situations arise when law enforcement officers are chasing suspects. Those chases may happen on the water (pursuing pirates, for example) or even in the air. However, the most common pursuits are car chases. In those, the police tend to be at a disadvantage, since the suspect may drive recklessly and also endanger other drivers while attempting to escape. Police drivers, by contrast, are bound to make every effort to avoid injury to people or property. However, police cars at different locations can communicate with one another by radio, greatly improving their chances of closing in on the suspect. Success is even more likely if a helicopter joins the pursuit. The helicopter pilot can keep police drivers informed of the suspect's movements, even when he or she suddenly leaves the car and tries to flee on foot. However, the high costs of running and flying helicopters often limits their use in most cases.

Thermal Imaging

Creatures and objects give off infrared radiation, which is beyond the range of light that the human eye can see. The amount of the radiation varies with the temperature of the object, so a device that measures radiation is effectively recording the heat that object produces. A thermographic camera produces an image in which a warm object, such as a human being, stands out against a cooler background. The image is processed to color-code the different temperature areas, from hottest to coldest, as white, yellow, orange, red, green, blue, and black.

A thermographic camera produced this image of a man, which is color-coded according to his body temperature.

In Hot Pursuit

Thermal imaging creates a photograph-like picture, based on the heat given off by people or objects, even on the darkest nights. The cameras used for thermal imaging are multipurpose crime fighting tools. An officer using a handheld thermographic camera can track suspects in the dark, seeing them without being seen. A thermographic camera penetrates walls and many other surfaces. Operated from an aircraft or helicopter, it can detect areas of abnormal heat — perhaps a decomposing body or a fire — even below the ground or inside a building.

Know Your Enemy

Away from the front line of policing, law enforcement authorities plan new strategies to fight crime. Crime prevention includes technological solutions such as CCTV, but also involves community efforts in which neighborhood "watch" groups keep an eye on their neighbors' properties.

Technology helps law enforcers anticipate where criminals will strike next. Since the 1960s, computerized geographic information systems (GIS) have been employed to analyze a wide range of data. The uses of GIS as a crime fighting tool include mapping areas in a city or region where crimes are most likely to occur. Police resources can then be concentrated where they are most needed.

 PROS: CRIME MAPPING

Using technology to identify high crime areas helps police detect and prevent crimes. By mapping the crime scenes, local road systems, and analyzing regional traffic patterns, police can identify the likely home of a criminal. Narrowing investigations in this way can save police time and lead to a quick arrest.

 CONS: CRIME MAPPING

Crime mapping encourages prejudices. Labeling certain areas and their inhabitants as criminally inclined can unfairly reduce property values.

A teenager wears an electronic monitor on his ankle. That monitor makes it possible for authorities to track his movements and ensure that he obeys the restrictions imposed on him.

Electronic Monitoring

Prisons are expensive to run. In the United States, they are also overcrowded. Some offenders have committed such serious crimes that they will spend decades in prison or may never be released. But many other former inmates will return to the community. One aspect of crime fighting is the effort made to prevent former prisoners from reoffending or becoming "career criminals." Such efforts include educational courses, job training, and helping drug offenders change their behavior so they can lead normal lives.

After their release, many former prisoners are regularly supervised by probation officers. In the 1980s, the United States pioneered a new electronic form of supervision, which has since been adopted by other countries. Offenders wear an electronic tracking device, typically in the form of a bracelet on the wrist or ankle. That device has a transmitter that uses Global Positioning Satellite (GPS) technology to signal the exact whereabouts of its wearer. An alternative system, used in the United Kingdom, tells a control center when the person is not at home. Most people are required to be indoors for set periods, usually overnight, as a condition of their release.

Electronic monitoring is most commonly used on nonviolent offenders. Some are sentenced to wear electronic monitors instead of going to prison. Others are inmates who were released early, before completing their sentences. The electronic monitor ensures they obey the conditions of their release. If they are out when they should not be, they will be rearrested and sent to prison.

Electronic Monitoring

VIEWPOINT

British Crown Court Judge David Mellor summarized the advantages of electronic monitoring in 2005:

"The sort of offender one has in mind is the tax-paying citizen who has behaved in a way that would normally be met with a short term of imprisonment. Instead of taking someone out of the community, so that he loses his job and the taxpayer has to support his family, and indeed support him in prison, it can be much more productive to lock him up at home."

➕ PROS: ELECTRONIC MONITORING

As an alternative sentence, electronic monitoring removes some of the pressure from overcrowded prisons. It gives former inmates the chance to rejoin their families and start readjusting to normal society.

➖ CONS: ELECTRONIC MONITORING

Some people wonder whether electronic monitoring affects crime rates. Arguably it weakens the justice system by creating the impression that offenders are getting off lightly. Some worry that possibly dangerous individuals are being released into the community.

The Future of Crime Fighting

Science and technology continually advance the tools needed to fight crime, though it seems likely that criminals will always find new ways to avoid detection. New crime-fighting technologies may emerge, but most future advancements will probably build upon existing methods.

Probabilities and Possibilities

New breakthroughs are often about making existing technology less expensive and easier to employ. One example is the handheld electronic notebooks that are now being used by some police forces. Those minicomputers link directly to police databases. However, when thinking about crime fighting in the future, it is important to distinguish between predictable developments and the many intriguing ideas that may or may not become realities. For example, in 2006 an Australian scientist claimed that within five years she would be able to extract such detailed information about facial features from DNA that experts could use it to construct a picture of a suspect or missing person!

Data and Identity

It seems safe to predict that government and law enforcement authorities will keep detailed records of increasing numbers of citizens. In the United Kingdom, some police officers have already called for a universal database that would contain details about the entire population. In the United States, where the Constitution guarantees citizens the right to own guns, some agencies believe that all weapons, not just those involved in a crime, should be recorded on the widely used Integrated Ballistics Identification System database.

If the present trend continues, law enforcement authorities will become ever more persistent in demanding proof of identity. The U.S. and U.K. governments intend to put laws in place that require all citizens to carry ID cards by about 2020, although opposition to those plans has been remarkably strong. However, if the ID cards prove easy to forge or use illegally, there are alternative technologies to identify individuals. Some of the most effective technologies are already in place to protect high-security areas and buildings. Scanners can use infrared light to measure the facial features of a person seeking entry and compare those results with a database on which the features of all authorized personnel are stored. Other devices scan human eyes to identify people through their eyes' unique features.

Eye-dentity

The iris is the colored area of the eye, surrounding the black pupil at its center. Every individual iris shows a unique arrangement of shapes, lines, and colors. That arrangement can be scanned by laser beam and recorded on a database. Whenever individuals enter a security-protected area, their irises can be scanned and compared with the database. Iris scanning is a rapid and apparently foolproof method of checking identity, though only practicable in situations where the equipment and database are available. Retinal scanning is a similar system, based on scanning the unique pattern of blood vessels at the back of the eyeball.

This woman's eye is being scanned by a biometric device that will identify patterns that are unique to her eye. Such patterns can be seen in both the iris and the retina. By comparing the scan with records already held, the device can tell whether she is who she claims to be.

+ PROS: PERSONAL RECORDS

Thorough record-keeping means more effective crime fighting. Organized and updated records can help identify victims and criminals. Keeping records has other benefits. In a medical emergency, an ID card enables medics to access a victim's medical history to begin treatment.

− CONS: PERSONAL RECORDS

ID cards and databases give governments information that can be misused to increase their power over citizens. Individuals may easily become victims of human or system errors, such as being wrongly placed in a database of potential terrorists. Such errors can be very difficult to correct.

Tracing and Tracking

Surveillance is likely to increase dramatically, helped by new technologies. That also means that governments and police will be watching the movements of almost all citizens and learning about formerly private activities.

In the United States and the United Kingdom, plans to monitor the e-mail, telephone, and Internet records of every person is ongoing. Tracking individuals is already commonplace and larger-scale operations will probably soon become possible. Some shopping malls record the movements of their customers. Although those systems do not currently record shoppers' identities, law enforcement officers may already be adapting such technology to their own requirements.

Future Crime Fighters

Police officers have long used specially-trained dogs to pick up a trail, find bodies, and detect drugs or chemicals used in bombs. However, recent research suggests that bees are more efficient, more reliable, and easier to train than dogs, which can become distracted or bored. Scientists teach bees by rewarding them with food whenever they recognize a smell. Digital cameras have shown bees "pointing" to register recognition by extending their proboscises, the tubes through which they suck nectar. Their ability to recognize the faintest odors is likely to make them highly successful crime fighters.

PROS: INCREASED SURVEILLANCE

Increased surveillance makes it easier to prevent or monitor illegal activities. Surveillance can make all the difference in combating terrorism.

CONS: INCREASED SURVEILLANCE

While the recent rise in terrorism justifies governments increasing their surveillance, security has to be balanced against citizens' rights to liberty and privacy. Many people fear that governments are becoming too powerful and intrusive.

The multiple screens of a CCTV surveillance system monitors activities in a public space. Surveillance enables police and security services to keep a close watch on people's movements.

Testing for the Truth

Science has yet to find a method to determine with certainty whether a person is telling the truth. A lie detector machine, the polygraph, has been widely used in the United States since 1921, and other countries also make use of it. But there are serious doubts about its reliability. Many U.S. courts do not allow polygraph results to be used as evidence. Sooner or later, scientists are likely to devise an improved form of lie detector. One avenue of research has been voice analysis. Some experiments suggest that it will be possible to analyze sound patterns in recorded speech, and that those will reveal when someone is lying.

Our increasing knowledge of how the brain works may provide a better solution. Changes in brain activity can already be scanned and, to some extent, matched to memories and feelings. In the future, scientists may be able to associate different kinds of brain activity with true and false statements made by a witness or suspect.

Taking the Test

A person who takes a lie detector test is wired to a device known as a polygraph. The operator then asks a series of questions. While that is happening, instruments measure the suspect's heart rate, blood pressure, perspiration, and breathing. When the subject replies to key questions, signs of stress such as an increased heart rate are taken to mean that he or she has lied. However, there may be other reasons why a person taking the test feels stressed — including fear of failure. For those reasons, many courts will not accept polygraph results unless other evidence supports their findings.

Speech Patterns

If terrorist threats persist, science and technology will almost certainly develop new ways to safeguard society. For example, in 2008, a Scottish student named Andrew McCallister won a prize for inventing a device to protect against car bombs. In response to a blast, the device inflates like a giant airbag, wrapping itself round an endangered building.

Terrorists, kidnappers, con artists, and hackers often warn police or threaten their intended victims about planned attacks with videos, recorded messages, or phone calls. Once a record of the criminal's voice exists, experts can convert the sounds into electrical currents and those currents

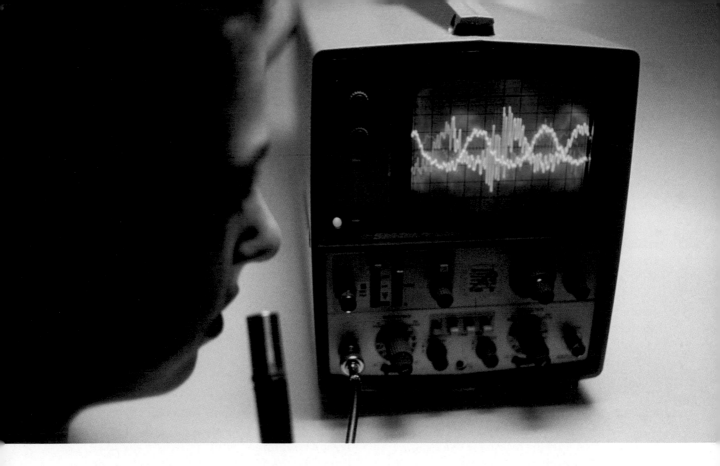

into graphs or voiceprints. According to voice analysts, differences in breathing, tone, accent, and other factors mean that each person's voice is as unique as his or her fingerprints. Like fingerprints, voiceprints can be compared with other samples and stored on a database. A number of cases have hinged on voiceprint evidence but not all experts believe it is 100 percent reliable. Future advancements are likely to change that.

In the future, voiceprinting may become a vital crime-fighting technique. This woman speaks into a microphone and her voice patterns are recorded.

 PROS: HIGH-TECH CRIME FIGHTING

Voiceprints and other high-tech crime fighting tools will help make the world safer and make it easier to identify and capture criminals.

 CONS: HIGH-TECH CRIME FIGHTING

Balancing security with liberty is not easy. Many new crime fighting techniques rely on large databases and increased monitoring of ordinary citizens.

GLOSSARY

archaeologist A specialist in the study of material remains from the past, such as bones or pottery

attenuated energy projectile (AEP) A nonlethal bullet used by police to put a person out of action without inflicting serious harm

autopsy An examination of a dead body to determine the cause of death

backscatter X-ray A form of X-ray used to check for hidden objects, weapons, or people

ballistics The science of firearms and bullets

biometric Describes the measuring of a living thing, often for identification purposes

carbon-14 dating A method of dating organic objects based on how much of a radioactive material, carbon-14, in them has decayed over time

clean suit A protective suit that prevents workers at a crime scene from coming into direct contact with evidence and contiminating it

closed-circuit television (CCTV) A form of television based on cameras that are positioned in public places to watch for criminal behavior

controlled explosion An explosion that destroys a dangerous object, such as a bomb, but is managed so that the least harm is done to surrounding people and property

conviction When an accused person is found guilty by a court

crime scene A place where a crime has been committed, or where useful evidence is discovered

CS gas (ortho-chlorobenzalmalononitrile) A chemical used in riot control; it causes irritation and watering of the eyes, which is why it is often called tear gas

database A catalog of computer files and information that can be managed and sorted to select specific material

eavesdropping Listening in to someone else's conversation

firewall A technology that protects a computer system against viruses and hackers

flight data recorder (FDR) A device in an aircraft that records all the readings from the instruments in the cockpit; also known as the black box

forensic To do with the law; for example, forensic medicine is concerned with the medical aspects of criminal and other legal cases

forgery An object that imitates another, for example, a bank note or a famous work of art, and which has been made with the intention of being passed off as the genuine article

gene A unit in a DNA sequence; it contains instructions that will determine some aspect of an individual's inherited characteristics, such as eye color

genocide The murder of an entire people, which is a crime of international law

geographic information systems (GIS) Computerized mapping systems

geophysics The scientific study of Earth's physical structure and processes

Global Positioning System (GPS) A method of fixing an exact position Earth that uses satellites to send and receives transmissions

ground-penetrating radar (GPR) A remote-sensing device based on the use of radio waves that can penetrate the ground; an unusual object that reflects them may be of interest to investigators

hacker A person who breaks into computer systems to steal valuable data or reshape it for malicious intentions

helix A winding spiral shape; DNA is arranged in the form of a double helix

identikit A method of constructing a picture of a person based on witness or other descriptions

informer A person, usually a criminal, who gives information to the police in return for money, better treatment, or a more lenient sentence

infrared A form of energy and light, invisible to the naked eye

Interpol The International Criminal Police Organization, established to encourage international cooperation in crime fighting

jury A group of people, not professional lawyers, who have been chosen to decide matters of fact, and of guilt or innocence, in a court of law

laser A device for producing intense beams of light

microchip An integrated circuit

microprocessor A microchip that contains the parts of a central processing unit; the "brains" of a computer

OC spray A chemical like CS gas that is used in riot control as it irritates the eyes and nose, causing tears and pain; also known as pepper spray

pathologist An expert in detecting and analyzing diseases and wounds

polygraph A machine that is used to try to establish whether someone is telling the truth; also known as a lie detector

post-mortem The surgical examination of a body after a sudden or suspicious death

probation A condition in which a criminal is out of prison but must report to a law enforcement officer and behave acceptably, following the rules of his or her probation agreement

profiler An expert who tries to understand the personality and behavior of a criminal in order to solve a case

radar A method of determining the position and movement of an object by sending out radio waves and measuring the time taken for them to be reflected back from the object

radioactivity The giving off of particles during the process of decay; some of those particles are harmful to human beings

saliva A liquid solution in the mouth, produced by the salivary glands and often used in DNA testing

scanning electron microscope An instrument that can magnify incredibly small objects, giving an image tens of thousands of times greater than the object's actual size; electron microscopes are used to examine tiny samples of physical evidence

GLOSSARY

smart card A plastic card containing a microchip that can process information; typical operations include security checks on credit or confirming the identity of an individual who attempts to enter a protected area

sonar A method of locating objects underwater by sending out bursts of sound waves and monitoring the echoes reflected by them

speed camera A camera that identifies and records speeding vehicles

suicide attack An attack carried out by individuals or groups who knowingly give up their lives in order to kill as many people as possible

surveillance Keeping watch on the activities of suspects or people in general

Taser A device that delivers an electric shock which temporarily stuns the victim and enables police to take him or her into custody

thermal imaging A method of creating pictures of an environment or person, based on differences in temperature

thermographic camera A camera used for thermal imaging

ultraviolet A form of energy and light, invisible to the naked eye

virus A computer program that infects a computer system and spreads, damaging other computers or entire computer networks

voiceprint A computerized record of the characteristics of an individual voice, used in identifying criminals

wiretapping Secretly listening in to telephone conversations

witness A person who has seen something that might be of value to the police in identifying a suspect or learning more about how a crime may have been committed

X-ray Invisible radiation used to penetrate body surfaces and soft tissue to produce an image

FURTHER INFORMATION

WEB SITES

CSI: Web Adventures
forensics.rice.edu
Test your skills on this interactive site based on the popular *CSI* TV series.

Discovery: Education
The Science of Forensics
school.discoveryeducation.com/lessonplans/
programs/forensics/index.html
The Discovery Channel web site for teachers and students includes activities and discussion ideas that explore how police officers use fingerprinting to solve crimes.

DNA Profiling Interactive
www.biotechnologyonline.gov.au/popups/
int_dnaprofiling.html
Discover more about interesting forensics cases and examine the evidence used to solve them, including DNA profiling.

Federal Bureau of Investigation Kids' Page
www.fbi.gov/fbikids.htm
This official site of the FBI explains the work of the agency to young people and includes games, stories, and other interactive activities.

Science News For Kids: Crime Lab
sciencenewsforkids.org/articles/20041215/
Feature1.asp
Get the inside scoop on how forensic scientists work on actual cases!

Publisher's note to educators and parents:

Our editors have carefully reviewed these web sites to ensure that they are suitable for children. Many web sites change, however, and we cannot guarantee that a site's future contents will continue to meet our high standards of quality and educational value. Be advised that children should be closely supervised whenever they access the Internet.

BOOKS

Baker, David. *CIA and FBI (Fighting Terrorism)*. Rourke (2005)

Ball, Jacqueline A. *Forensics*. Gareth Stevens Publishing (2003)

Cooper, Chris. *Eyewitness: Forensic Science*. Dorling Kindersley (2008)

Denega, Danielle M. *Have You Seen This Face? The Work of Forensic Artists*. Franklin Watts (2007)

Gifford, Clive. *Crimebusters: How Science Fights Crime*. Oxford University Press (2007)

Hopping, Lorraine Jean, and Barbara Davis. *Investigating a Crime Scene*. Gareth Stevens Publishing (2007)

Horn, Geoffrey M. *Crime Scene Investigator*. Gareth Stevens Publishing (2008)

Houck, Max M. *Trace Evidence*. Facts on File (2009)

Hunter, William. *DNA Analysis*. Mason Crest (2005)

Marzilli, Alan. *The Internet and Crime*. Chelsea House Publishers (2009)

Morrison, Yvonne. *The DNA Gave It Away! Teens Solve Crime*. Children's Press (2007)

Piper, Ross. *Fingerprinting Wizards: The Secrets of Forensic Science*. Capstone Press (2009)

Platt, Richard. *Forensics (Kingfisher Knowledge)*. Kingfisher (2005)

Shone, Rob. *Crime Scene Investigators*. Rosen Publishing (2008)

INDEX

Page numbers in **BOLD** refer to illustrations and charts.

airport security 27, 28–29, 31
al-Qaeda 26
arson 40
attenuated energy projectiles (AEPs) 47, 48
autopsies 6

backscatter X-rays 28, **29**
ballistics 8, **8**, 54
bees 56
biometric passports 27
blackmail 20
blood 4
  as evidence 4, 6, 9, 42, **43**
  types 4
body identification 34, 36–37
bomb disposal 32, **32**
bombs 14, **30**, 31, 32, **32**, 56, 58
Borden, Lizzie 4
Brady, Ian 37
bugs 18–19, **19**, 20
Bulger, James 22
burglary 18, 20

casts 7
clean suits 5, **5**
closed-circuit television (CCTV) 20–23, **21**, 27, 31, 33, 51, **57**
computers 10–17, **12**, **13**, **15**, 24, 27, 34, 39, 51
  crime 14–17
  hacking 15–17
  image enhancement 10
  viruses 16–17
crime scenes 4–5, **5**, 6, 7, 37, 38, 42, 45
CS gas (tear gas) 48, 49
CSI (Crime Scene Investigation) 8, 9

databases 10–14, 24, 38, 42, 45, 54, 56, 59
DNA 41, **41**, 54
  databases 45
  testing 41–5, **43**, **44**
drugs 9, 28, 52, 56

eavesdropping 18–20
electronic tagging **52**, 53
electrostatic device (ESDA) 6
e-mails 10, 15, 16, 27, 33, 56
facial reconstruction 3, 35, **35**
fingerprints 6–7, **7**, 10–11, 14, 59

firearms 8, **46**, 47, 48
flight data recorders (black boxes) 33
forensic sculptors **35**
forgery 6, 9

geographic information systems (GIS) 51

hacking 15–17, **16**
handwriting 6
Hindley, Myra 37
Holton, Rudolph 43
hostages 40

identification techniques
  ballistics 54
  dental 34
  DNA testing 42
  electronic 27
  reconstruction 34, 35, 35
identikits 38–39, **39**, 40, 54
identity (ID) cards 27, 28, 34, 55, 56
identity theft 15
Integrated Ballistics Identification System 54
Internet 10, 14, 16, 17, 56
  crime 14–17
Interpol 13
iris scanning 55, **55**

kidnapping 6, 9, 22, 40, 58

laboratory tests 6, 8–9, 42
lie detector *see* polygraph
line searches 36
Lockerbie, Scotland 33

McKinnon, Gary **16**
microscopes 9
  comparison 9
  scanning electron 9
missing people 36–37
murder 4, 9, 11, 34, 36, 37, 40, 43

nonlethal weapons 47–49
nuclear devices 31
OC spray (pepper spray) 48

pathologists 6, 34
police **5**, 8, **11**, **13**, **25**, **36**, **43**, **46**, **48**
  armed 47, 48

car chases 49
  databases 10–14, 24, 42, 54
  law enforcement methods 13, 14, 46–53
polygraph 58
prisons 52–53
profiling 40

rape 40
retinal scanning 55, **55**
robbery 9, 14

security barriers **30**, 30–31
shoplifting 20
Simpson, O.J. 9
smart cards 27
sniffer dogs 31, **36**, 56
speed cameras 24–25, **25**
speeding 23–25
suicide attacks 27, 30
surveillance 18–25, **21**, 56–57, **57**
  motorists 23–25
  protests **22**
Sutcliffe, Peter William 11, **11**

Tasers 47, 49
terrorism 14, 21, 26–33, 56
terrorist attacks 26–27, 28, 33
theft 9
thermal imaging **50**, 50–51

vandalism 20
voiceprints 56, 57, **57**

war crimes 9, 34
water cannons 48, **48**, 49
wiretaps 18
witness statements 4, 33, 38
World Trade Center **26**, 27

About the Author
Nathaniel Harris was educated at University College in Oxford, United Kingdom. He taught and worked in publishing before becoming a full-time writer. He has written many books about history and current events.

About the Consultant
Miles Hudson is a high school science teacher and author of many science and physics textbooks for young people.

Harris County Public Library
Houston, Texas